BERKSHIRE
AIRFIELD.
SECOND WC   ^R

Robin J. Brooks

COUNTRYSIDE BOOKS
NEWBURY, BERKSHIRE

First published 2014
© Robin J. Brooks 2014

COUNTRYSIDE BOOKS
3 Catherine Road
Newbury
Berkshire
RG14 7NA

To view our complete range of books, please visit us at
www.countrysidebooks.co.uk

Some of the text and photographs in this book appeared
in the publication *Thames Valley Airfields in the Second World War*,
which was published in 2000.

ISBN 978 1 84674 329 0

The cover painting is by Colin Doggett and shows
a female pilot of the Air Transport Auxiliary at
White Waltham aerodrome.

Produced by The Letterworks Ltd., Reading
Typeset by Mac Style Ltd.
Printed by Berforts Information Press, Oxford

CONTENTS

The Air Transport Auxiliary, White Waltham. A Stirling bomber dwarfs its pilot, Flt Capt Joan Hughes. An outstanding woman aviator, she joined the ATA in January 1940, at the age of 21. She became the only woman pilot to instruct on all classes of aircraft and delivered 75 four-engined bombers herself. After the war she remained as a flying instructor at White Waltham until 1961. She died in 1993. (Photo courtesy of West London Aero Club)

INTRODUCTION

Although some distance from the Channel coast and the main battle area, the airfields of Berkshire still played a vital part in the war effort. For most of the war they were mainly used in training and troop carrying roles. From 1943, the USAAF arrived to carry out much of this sterling work. From bases such as Aldermaston and Greenham Common, vast armies were transported in troop carrying aircraft and gliders, to begin the assault on mainland Europe that would eventually bring victory. For the RAF, many Operational Training Units were stationed within the region, ensuring that Bomber Command always had a surplus of crews. It was a time when the skies above Berkshire were filled with the roar of aircraft engines.

There are many stories of courage and heroism in this book. Of particular interest are the feats of the Air Transport Auxiliary whose headquarters were at White Waltham aerodrome, near Maidenhead. Although both men and women flew with the ATA it will be for ever linked with the latter, who proved themselves highly skilled aviators; see the photograph opposite.

The civilian population also came to experience war at its most devastating with bombing raids on some of the towns. They were to endure dreadful attacks with civilian deaths and injuries. Reading and Newbury both suffered disastrous daylight raids on 10th February, 1943.

In this volume I have attempted to bring to the reader the feel of that time. The units that flew from the airfields, the death and destruction and the horror of war are all recorded. In this respect, I dedicate the following pages to all those who died or suffered through those traumatic times.

Robin J. Brooks

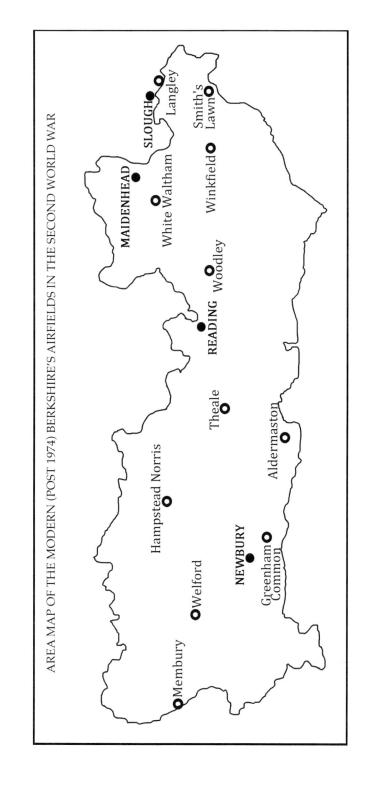

AREA MAP OF THE MODERN (POST 1974) BERKSHIRE'S AIRFIELDS IN THE SECOND WORLD WAR

SLOUGH
Langley
Smith's Lawn
MAIDENHEAD
White Waltham
Winkfield
Woodley
READING
Theale
Aldermaston
Hampstead Norris
NEWBURY
Welford
Greenham Common
Membury

I
SETTING
THE SCENE

When the armistice of the First World War was signed, thoughts of any future wars faded from the public mind. Known as, 'the war to end all wars', the conflict had had little effect on the rural county of Berkshire, with the exception of the men who had left to fight in France and Belgium. The advent of the aeroplane and the formation of the Royal Naval Air Service and the Royal Flying Corps between 1914 and 1918 left an impression on many that the aeroplane was just a killing machine. Thus, many of the aircraft factories such as Sopwith, Avro and de Havilland saw a downturn in demand and manufacture. It was not until late 1919 that flying for pleasure began to become acceptable to the general public of Berkshire.

This was partly due to the exploits of the innovative Berkshire Aviation Company. Based at East Hanney, (in what was then Berkshire and is now Oxfordshire) the company was set up by brothers Fred and John Holmes, together with air pioneer Alan Cobham. Starting off with an Avro 504K, which they had bought for £600 from a war surplus depot, they toured Berkshire and the surrounding counties offering people short air experience flights, known as 'joyriding'. The first joyriding flight took place

Construction of an airfield 'somewhere in the South East'. The photo shows the laying of a hard runway. (IWM)

on 27th May 1919, near Newbury, and continued until a forced landing damaged the Avro beyond economical repair. With their insurance claim settled, the company purchased another aircraft and continued their flights of pleasure until 1922, by which time a total of over 34,000 people had been introduced to the experience of flying, with further aircraft bought and pilots employed.

After one year with the company, Alan Cobham left to join the de Havilland Aircraft Co. He toured the country offering National Aviation Days, visiting Newbury and Reading in 1932, as he brought aviation to even more people. This period between the wars became known as 'the halcyon days of flying', but with the signs of unrest permeating from Germany once again the last tour of the National Aviation Day took place in 1935. Not until 1946 would flying for pleasure be allowed once again.

When the Second World War broke out, main fighter aerodromes were situated closer to the capital, and Berkshire was to become a county more associated with bomber training units (OTUs), Transport Command and the United States Army Air Force. The Battle of Britain in 1940 had little effect on Berkshire but with the

The Nissen hut is still to be seen on many of Berkshire's wartime airfields.

planning and eventual success of 'Operation Overlord', the 1944 D-Day assault upon occupied Europe, many of the airfields saw as much air activity in a few months as some did throughout the duration of the war. One of these airfields was Aldermaston, for ever associated since the end of the war with a far more devastating and sinister type of warfare – nuclear.

When the Aldermaston site was chosen in 1941, it was planned as an Operational Training Unit (OTU) for bombers. However, the intended Wellingtons never arrived and the base was handed over to the USAAF for troop carrying movements. At the end of the war it was handed back to the RAF but used by BOAC as a training base. In 1950 it was converted to be used by the Atomic Weapons Research Establishment (now AWE).

Greenham Common on the other hand was used almost exclusively by the USAAF. Surveyed at the same time as Aldermaston as a possible satellite to that base, again the RAF never arrived and it was handed over to the Americans for the planning of the D-Day operations. Greenham Common was heavily used over the D-Day period when C-47 Dakotas towing

9

Practising for D-Day – troops ready to embark on Whitley bombers. Several Berkshire airfields saw such scenes. (SE Newspapers)

Hadrian and Horsa gliders were some of the first aircraft over Normandy during the 5th to the 6th June, 1944. In 1945, the base was returned to the RAF and Technical Training Command, but it quickly fell out of use when declared surplus to requirements. However, the Cold War of the 1950s brought further American use, including the storage of cruise missiles in the 1980s. The base then became the subject of intense anti-nuclear campaigns but with the glasnost period of the late 1980s, the Americans left. Today Greenham Common is an open area of heathland, a haven for wildlife and popular with local dog walkers and birdwatchers. It also includes a large area called Greenham Business Park.

Membury, between Newbury and Swindon, was another airfield used by the USAAF though this time for reconnaissance aircraft. Originally intended for bomber use, it was occupied by the Americans flying a varied collection of aircraft such as Havocs, Mustangs and the Douglas C-47 Dakota. Membury was taken back by the British in 1947, to be used by RAF Transport Command until it was finally decommissioned. Much of the site today is given over to light industry but parts of the original runways are still used for leisure flights.

The last of the USAAF bases in Berkshire was Welford. Again, this was planned as a bomber OTU, but was taken over by the USAAF for troop transport. It returned to the RAF in 1945 and was used by Transport Command but was reduced to care and maintenance a year later. Part of the site was reopened under Maintenance Command in August 1952 and the site continues to be used as a storage base for ordnance of various kinds.

For the RAF the county supported Great Shefford as a relief or emergency landing ground but it saw little use. Theale was the base for No. 26 Elementary Flying Training School using the standard trainer of the period, the Tiger Moth. The base served this purpose throughout the war only being placed under care and maintenance on June 30, 1945. An Air Cadet Gliding School remained until 1948 when the MOD sold the site to a gravel quarrying company.

The remaining Berkshire airfields were mainly used for training. Woodley, which opened in 1939, followed this role, but with the

One of the nuclear silos on Greenham Common where the cruise missiles were stored. The GAMA Complex was one of six built in Europe to house ground launched cruise missiles.

11

addition of the Miles Aircraft factory producing the Magister trainer. It was also the home of No. 8 Elementary and Reserve Flying Training School. From 1946 to 1951, Woodley was used as a communications station but all flying ceased in 1953 with the site being given over to housing.

The final military site is Smith's Lawn. There had been a grass airfield on the site since the 1920s for the private use of the Prince of Wales but Vickers Armstrong used the airfield from 1940 for building special versions of the Wellington. Situated in a corner of Windsor Great Park, it was ideally located for the quick evacuation of the royal family should this be necessary in the event of a German invasion. It became a storage depot for Vickers Warwick bombers until the end of the war, and is now parkland.

So the scene was set for Berkshire and wartime. Alongside the county, Middlesex, curving around the western side of the capital, contained the important fighter station of Northolt. Although strictly outside the confines of this book, it is worthy of a mention. The Second World War saw it develop rapidly as a military airfield within No. 11 Group. It became home to many Polish squadrons during the six years of war and after that it became a major transport hub. Today, Northolt has survived all the reductions put upon military bases and is the home of the Queen's Flight together with a variety of civilian, corporate and VIP flights from all over the world.

Mention should also be made of RAF Uxbridge, which was the wartime headquarters of No. 11 Group, Fighter Command. From this underground establishment the Battle of Britain was controlled and fought, bringing victory to the RAF in that decisive conflict. Alongside Air Chief Marshal Sir Hugh Dowding, Air Vice-Marshal Keith Park and other senior controllers, it was their strategy that enabled the battle to be won. Today the site has been sold for development although the underground operations room has been given listed status and will be kept as a museum and memorial to those days and nights of peril.

Across the border in Buckinghamshire, the USAAF used Cheddington, near Aylesbury, as a crew and aircraft replacement centre when it was found to be unsuitable for full operational use.

Air Vice-Marshal Sir Keith Rodney Park, Commander of No 11 Group, Fighter Command during the Battle of Britain. (IWM)

Smaller airfields at Booker, Little Horwood, Westcott and Wing were training bases, with glider pilot training being carried out at Thame. The totally secret and vitally important location known to all now as 'Station X' also comes within that county. Bletchley Park, on the main railway line from London, was the intelligence centre for the war as day after day and night after night, scientists and mathematicians struggled to break German and Japanese military codes, thus giving British intelligence the edge on the enemy. The German machine known as 'Enigma' allowed them to do this without the enemy knowing that their messages had been intercepted. A German commander after the war admitted that, 'It was intelligence that won the war.' Now Bletchley Park is a national museum and very much open to the public.

Today Berkshire is a wonderful county in which to live. There are still signs of its war if you look carefully, and the memories of its people from that era will last for ever.

13

2

ALDERMASTON

One of the targets since the 1950s for 'Ban the Bomb' protestors has been Aldermaston airfield, a few miles south-east of Aldermaston village. With its closure by the Ministry of Civil Aviation in 1950, it became the Atomic Weapons Research Establishment. Today, it is known as the Atomic Weapons Establishment and is at the forefront of the UK nuclear deterrence programme. Before this however, it was a major troop-carrying airfield.

As with many airfields in the area, Aldermaston was built and developed as a bomber OTU in 1941. Ready by 1st July 1942, it became part of No 92 Group but was not used in its intended role. Instead it was allocated to the USAAF. The arrival of the 60th Troop Carrier Group comprising the 10th, 11th, 12th and 28th Troop Carrier Squadrons was completed by September 1942 and Aldermaston became Airfield No 467 on 20th October.

C-47s soon began to arrive but with the opening of the second front in North Africa, the 60th were transferred to the 12th Air Force. 'Operation Torch' began in October 1942 and on 6th November, the C-47s left for Portreath in Cornwall before going overseas. By this time, four 'T' Type hangars had been constructed on the main airfield and in the vicinity of one of the dispersal areas another shed had been built. This was taken over by Vickers in July 1943 for Spitfire assembly and when complete, the aircraft were test-flown from Aldermaston. This assembly plant was to continue until the end of the war was in sight.

14

With the departure of the Americans, Aldermaston returned very briefly to RAF control. A detachment of No 3 GTS arrived in late 1942, eventually turning out to be the only RAF unit to ever use the base. They stayed for a brief period before the next American unit arrived. The 315th TCG came in on 12th December 1942 with their C-47s and C-53s arriving in February 1943. Consisting of the 34th and 43rd TCS, they soon received their own gliders in the form of Waco CG-4A Hadrians.

Unlike British gliders which were of wooden construction, the Hadrian was made of wood with a steel tubular fuselage. It carried a crew of two and could accommodate 13 troops, far fewer than the British gliders. Apart from on Sicily, Hadrians were not used by the RAF, but they were one of the standard gliders used by the USAAF.

With the gliders arriving in May, the 315th sent some on detachment to assist in the Sicilian landings. During their absence, the group was transferred to the 9th Air Force and moved over to Welford in November 1943.

Aldermaston now became the home of the 370th Fighter Group and the 71st Fighter Wing headquarters. The 370th had become one of the three Lightning-equipped fighter units of the 9th Air Force. With its distinctive twin boom tail, the Lockheed Lightning performed a wide variety of missions in every war theatre and was to eventually destroy more Japanese aircraft in the Pacific than any other fighter. It was also intended to use the type in RAF service but after taking a delivery of three, they rejected it and subsequently cancelled an order for 524 Mk.IIs. These were taken over by the USAAF, some of which eventually found their way to Aldermaston.

Yet again the stay was shortlived and it was not until 3rd March 1944 that Aldermaston really came into its own. By then the 9th Air Force Air Support Command headquarters had exchanged names with the 19th ASC. Personnel and equipment stayed the same, just the name changed. This allowed the 434th TCG to arrive from Fulbeck. The four squadrons, 71st, 72nd, 73rd and 74th, immediately began intense training with their complement of C-47s. This was carried out in conjunction with the 101st Airborne Division, the intensity increasing as D-Day approached.

As the men and women prepared for the great day, a vast cloak of security was thrown around the airfield. A BBC commentator at the time captured this tense atmosphere:

A Jeep towing a troop-carrying glider to the runway, where it will be hitched to a C-47 or C-53, May 1943, 315th Troop Carrier Group. The glider could

carry 16 men, or one jeep and 6 men, or one 37 mm anti-tank gun and crew, while the towing ship carried 18 airborne troops. (Signal Corps)

'This base and many more like it are sealed because we have been told the answers. The answers to the questions that the whole world had been asking for two years or more. Where and how and when! Troops swarmed around last night, strong, healthy, formidable men. Many of them going into battle for the first time.'

At dawn on 6th June, the C-47s towed 52 Hadrians carrying men of the 81st Airborne AA Battalion. Once again, the BBC were there to record the historic moment:

'The first aircraft that is going to lead in the early hours of tomorrow morning is turning at the end of the tarmac to make its take-off. A graceful machine, its wingtip lights shining red and green over the heads of the smaller figures of people on the aerodrome watching it take off. Taking off from here, loaded with parachutists and taking with it perhaps the hopes and the fears of millions of people in this country who sleep tonight, not knowing that this mighty operation is taking place. There she goes now, the first aircraft leaving. Faster and faster and up into the air as we wave far below and wish them Godspeed and good luck.'

Supplies are loaded aboard a C-47 ready to drop to the troops on D-Day Plus 1.

Ready for D-Day Plus 1, the Waco Hadrian gliders are lined up at Aldermaston awaiting the troops of the Carrier Group. (After the Battle)

It was still moonlight when the first C-47 crossed the coast. Encountering a lot of flak, several aircraft were caught by accurate gun-fire but 49 aircraft reached the drop zone and released their gliders. Several failed to make the exact landing site and landed among trees a mile inland from the Omaha Beach. This area was infested with enemy artillery and many good men who landed by air and sea never returned. The losses were high, but eventually a bridgehead was established.

For days after the initial assault, the group continued to drop supplies as well as training for the next big operation, Arnhem. On 17th September for 'Operation Market Garden', the 434th TCG carried the 82nd Airborne Division to Nijmegen followed by further supply drops. This continued into 1945 when they flew to a new base in mainland Europe at Mourmelon-le-Grand on 12th February.

Lieutenant General Brereton, Commander 1st Allied Airborne Army, talking at Aldermaston to Colonel Whiteacre, CO of 434th Troop Carrier Group, and Colonel Joseph Harper of 327th Glider Infantry Regiment of 101st Airborne Division. This is 18th September 1944 – the second day of 'Operation Market Garden'. (National Archives via After the Battle)

With victory finally in sight, the 9th Air Force handed Aldermaston back to the RAF. A branch of Technical Training Command arrived, together with No 25 (RCAF) Aircrew Holding Unit for the purpose of recruiting men to continue the fight against Japan. Disbanding in December 1945, Aldermaston entered a period of Care and Maintenance which was to continue until 9th May 1946 when BOAC arrived and the airfield was given over to civil aviation. Dakotas, Oxfords and Yorks now used the facilities, later joined by large aircraft such as the Halifax. On 1st January 1947, Airways Training Ltd formed a school on the site, but by November 1948 this had closed and the number of movements from Aldermaston began to dwindle. For a short period, Eagle Aviation were based there but when the airfield was relinquished by the Ministry of Civil Aviation in April 1950, the Atomic Weapons Research Establishment moved in.

When the nuclear strikes on Hiroshima and Nagasaki had brought Japanese resistance to an end in 1946, a new type of warfare had been unleashed, one that was to threaten the very existence of mankind. The shape of the Cold War had been confirmed in 1949 and Britain, along with America, was about to enter the nuclear age.

Two photographs of post-war Aldermaston showing the large wartime hangars. (Aeroplane via F. Cheeseman)

21

Resources were put into a programme to develop the weapons of mass destruction by scientists such as Professors Penney, Hinton and Cockcroft. An atomic bomb was first tested and exploded in 1952 in the Monte Bello Islands in Australia. This prompted the Campaign for Nuclear Disarmament to hold rallies all over the country. The first Aldermaston March organised by CND was in Easter 1958 when demonstrators marched for four days from Trafalgar Square, London, to the AWRE site at Aldermaston.

Many of the wartime buildings have now gone and have given way to a housing estate on the south of the airfield. Though the Cold War has been down-graded, research development into weapons of mass destruction still continues at AWE in Aldermaston.

The ultimate result of the work at Aldermaston post-war. The explosion of the British atomic bomb in the Monte Bello Islands, Australia. (Crown copyright)

3
GREENHAM COMMON

Intended for use as a bomber Operational Training Unit like so many other sites in Berkshire, Greenham Common was eventually to become a USAAF base. Lying on a ridge between the Kennet and Enborne rivers, construction started early in 1942. It was to be one of the larger airfields with a main runway 4,800 feet in length and two secondary runways, one being 4,050 feet and the other 3,300 feet. Several minor roads crossing the ridge had to be closed to accommodate the site with the main Newbury-Basingstoke road being allowed to remain open, but fitted with barriers for closing when aircraft were operational. Even then, the airfield was found to be not large enough and a period of further expansion took place during late 1942. The accommodation area was constructed around the eastern perimeter with two T2 hangars being erected together with a technical site and a 27-pan hardstanding perimeter area.

Though the airfield was not completely finished, the headquarters staff of the 51st Troop Carrier Wing arrived from the USA in September 1942. With 'Operation Torch', the invasion of French North Africa, taking place in October, the 51st TCW moved to North Africa the following month. Responsibility for Greenham Common was transferred back to the RAF and No 70 Group. The arrival of No 15 Air Firing Unit and No 1511 Beam Approach Training Flight on 28th April 1943 brought the Airspeed

Oxford to Greenham. The RAF's first twin-engined monoplane advanced trainer, it became the workhorse of the force, being used in a wide variety of essential roles.

For five months the Oxfords were the only aircraft stationed at Greenham but when the airfield was again required by the Americans, they had to move elsewhere. An area adjacent to the main airfield at Crookham Common was also requisitioned as an assembly plant for the Waco gliders that were arriving in crates from the USA. Once assembled, they were towed by road onto the airfield proper before being taken to other airfields. As the plans for the invasion of Europe developed, assembly increased from 15 to 50 a day just prior to 'Overlord'.

On 1st October 1943, Greenham Common became USAAF Station 486 and was handed over to the 9th Air Force for the use of, not troop aircraft, but fighters. Duly, the personnel of the 354th Fighter Group arrived to find that they were to be given the new P-51D Mustang. One of the most outstanding fighter aircraft of the

American troops relaxing in the period leading up to D-Day. (SE Newspapers)

24

war, its performance was superior to that of any other American fighter and it was one of many American fighters to be used by the RAF. The aircraft used by the 354th were powered by the British Rolls-Royce Merlin engine, this proving superior to the earlier American Allison engine. As a fighter, the Mustang was to escort the large American bomber formations that were to bomb Germany by day, in the process becoming known as the 'Little Friends'. The 354th, the 'Pioneer Mustang Group', worked up on the type for a week before moving to Boxted in Essex.

They were replaced by the HQ of the 70th Fighter Wing, who were in turn replaced by the 100th Fighter Wing on 6th December 1943. In a period of rapid change, the new year saw the 368th Fighter Group arrive bringing the first Republic P-47 Thunderbolts to fly from Greenham Common. Affectionately known as 'the Jug', the aircraft was first introduced to the European Theatre of Operations on 10th March 1943. The size and weight of the aircraft dismayed the pilots of the USAAF, but the addition of drop tanks and an increased size of internal tanks turned it into a suitable long-range, high altitude aircraft. Yet again, they only stayed to briefly work up on the P-47 before moving on to Chilbolton in Hampshire (see *Hampshire Airfields in the Second World War*). They did, however, carry out one mission from Greenham, that of flying to the French coast on 14th March 1944. No combat took place and all 48 aircraft of the group returned safely to base. A reorganisation of the command dictated that Greenham Common was to become a troop carrier base. Accordingly, no further fighters were to be stationed there as it became the home of the 438th TCG on 16th March 1944. The four squadrons incorporated in the 438th were the 87th, 88th, 89th and the 90th, all flying the familiar C-47 or C-53. As with all the other troop carrier bases, there began a period of intense glider training. Considerable changes had to be made to the airfield to allow for mass stream take-offs, the quickest way to get such great formations of aircraft airborne. The 438th was earmarked to lead the airborne forces to the dropping zones on 5th/6th June and consequently, the eve of the invasion saw a string of top military personnel at the base, including the Supreme Commander, General Dwight Eisenhower.

25

Troops of the 101st Airborne Division seated in their glider ready for take-off at Greenham Common during D-Day rehearsals. (War Dept, Washington)

Preparing to board their glider.

General Eisenhower was a frequent visitor to Greenham around the D-Day period.

At 10.45 pm on 5th June 1944, 81 aircraft and their gliders took off from Greenham Common carrying the men of the 101st Airborne Division. The Channel crossing was uneventful and the gliders were cast off soon after midnight in the area of Carentan. Returning to Greenham Common, the C-47s were later tasked with towing Hadrian and Horsa gliders containing the troop reinforcements. Sadly, a C-47 and a C-53 were lost to heavy flak but for this and other work, the Group received a Distinguished Unit Citation.

With 'Overlord' a success, three squadrons of the 438th – the 87th, 88th and 89th – were deployed to Canino in Italy to take part in the invasion of southern France. The 90th Squadron moved over to Welford for the duration, all the units returning to Greenham on 24th August 1944.

It was 'Operation Market Garden' that the 438th were next tasked with. In common with all the other troop-carrying bases in the area, 90 aircraft dropped paratroops of the 101st Airborne

27

An insulated container of blood is made ready for despatch in a Dakota to the battlefields of Normandy on 14th June 1944 at Greenham Common. (War Dept, Washington)

Division near Eindhoven on 17th September. For the next two days, further glider missions were flown, the 19th being a day of several losses. With 40 aircraft towing gliders and leaving Greenham Common in difficult weather, one C-47 was hit by flak and lost whilst several gliders cast off too early and were also lost. The next few days were given over to dropping supplies to the troops below, with a glider-towing mission on 23rd September being the last for the 438th. With the rapid advances in Europe, they moved to Prosnes in France in February 1945.

The assembly of the Waco gliders continued for a time, the final number being over 4,000. This ceased with the ending of the

28

war and Greenham Common was handed back to the RAF and Transport Command. In August a transfer to Technical Training Command brought to the base the sound of raw recruits being given drill instruction, perhaps an ignominious end for such a large transport airfield. On 1st June 1946, Greenham Common was declared surplus to requirements and quickly fell into disrepair.

It would have continued this way but, as the Cold War developed in the 1950s, it was one of several airfields loaned to the USAF and was totally redeveloped including new runways to accommodate B-29s, B-36s, B-47s and ultimately B-52 strategic bombers. In the 1980s, huge additional silos and storage bunkers were built as 96 cruise missiles with nuclear warheads were sited there.

This resulted in many demonstrations and the setting up of the famous 'Women's Peace Camp' around the entrance to the base. The protest grew with women from the UK and abroad arriving to spend time at the camp. As it gained recognition, journalists from around the world came to report on the protest.

The cruise missiles were finally removed from Greenham Common following the signing of the USA-USSR Intermediate

A critical cargo of medical supplies for Normandy is rushed to a waiting plane. (National Archives)

29

Greenham Common's Grade II listed Control Tower is being converted into a visitor centre to ensure the historical importance of the former airbase is not forgotten.

Nuclear Forces Treaty in 1987, and in 1992 the base was declared surplus to requirements and closed. Today, much of the airfield has been sold to developers. The majority of the runway has been removed and the area passed back as public open space, although there are reminders of the site's former use, the most obvious being the GAMA complex, where the cruise missiles were stored.

On 12th December 1944, 31 American paratroopers and 2 pilots were killed when their glider crashed at the airbase shortly after take off. Three days later, two B-17 Flying Fortress Bombers collided, killing all but 2 of the 18 crew. Every December, a memorial service is held at the business park to remember the American servicemen who died in these accidents.

4

MEMBURY

If 'Operation Market Garden' had been the success that was hoped for, the war may well have finished one year earlier. In the words of Field Marshal Montgomery, 'it could be the springboard for a powerful full-blooded thrust to the heart of Germany.' In contrast however, General Bittrich of the German Army said, 'Almost before the British had touched the ground, we were ready to defeat them.'

'Market Garden' was General Montgomery's bold and imaginative plan for an armoured and airborne thrust across Holland to outflank the German defences. After much argument, he persuaded General Eisenhower to go along with his project which incorporated the US 1st Army, the British 21st Army Group and the Allied Airborne Army. The object was to initially capture five major bridges: two over canals and three over rivers. It was an ambitious plan and if successful, the advantages could have included a swift end to the war. Montgomery's aim was to drop three airborne divisions to seize the bridges on the Eindhoven-Arnhem road to enable units of the 21st Army Group to outflank the Siegfried Line. On Sunday morning, 17th September 1944, 'Market Garden' began.

The first part went well with the US 101st Airborne Division capturing the two southern bridges. At Arnhem, things had not gone right from the start. The British 1st Airborne had been dropped a long way from the town and had met fierce German resistance. The American Airborne units also found that the Nijmegen bridge was strongly held. The British Paratroops, aiming for Arnhem found their way blocked by a superior force of Germans and were eventually overwhelmed. The hoped-for objective to secure a Rhine bridgehead at Arnhem had not been achieved and many good men were to sacrifice their lives. For Membury, whose glider units had participated fully in the invasion, it was a sad day.

As with many of the bases taken over by the Americans, Membury began life as a bomber OTU. Situated three miles south-west of Lambourn, it was authorised as an airfield in May 1941. It had the typical bomber airfield layout, this being a main south-west/north-east runway of 4,554 feet together with two subsidiary runways. Four T2 hangars, a technical and a domestic area completed the set-up. From the beginning it had been earmarked for Bomber Command and was in fact accepted from the contractors by No 91 Group. However, the establishment of the USAAF in the UK meant that several bomber airfields would be needed for their use, one of them being Membury. By 21st August 1942, the headquarters personnel from the 8th Group Air Support Command had arrived and designated the airfield as Station 466.

By September the units at the base comprised the 3rd Photographic Group, the 675th Observation Group and the 153rd Liaison Squadron. Quite a mixture! The aircraft used in all these roles were a few camera-equipped B-17s together with some Piper Cubs. The Photographic Unit had left by September as the first Spitfires to be flown from Membury arrived.

About a thousand Spitfires of various marks were used by units of the USAAF. The 67th Tactical Reconnaissance Group flew the Spitfire V and arrived at Membury in the autumn. Whilst the American Eagle Squadrons had flown the Spitfire during the Battle of Britain as part of Fighter Command, with the creation of the 8th Air Force, all the Eagle Squadrons became absorbed into that command.

Although the 8th had by this time established itself in the UK under the command of Major General Carl Spaatz, it was unable to accomplish much until the spring of 1943. This was due to the fact that many of the men and machines destined for the 8th were conscripted to the 12th Air Force during 'Operation Torch', the landings in North Africa.

Early in 1943, a number of target-towing Douglas A-20 Havocs were flown into Membury to be used in conjunction with the Spitfires. The station at this time was basically used as a training airfield and even the appearance of No 19 Squadron on 10th March 1943 with their Spitfire VBs and VCs did little to change the role. Flying in from Middle Wallop, they stayed for three days before going back to the Hampshire airfield.

In June, the unit was renamed the 67th Reconnaissance Group and with the new title came a succession of fighter sweeps over France. The Americans flew in company with the RAF on these sorties and even the Havoc crews got to go on operations when not target towing. Over the next two months, very little changed at Membury until the 67th RG moved over to Middle Wallop.

Membury was now to be extended as it became the 6th Tactical Air Depot, 9th Air Force. No further extension of the main runway was possible and so the secondary stretch running north/south was lengthened to 6,000 feet. During this work it was further decided that Membury would become the home of a Troop Carrier Group, necessitating a move from RAF control to the 9th Air Force on 22nd February 1944.

The 9th had been established in England on 16th October 1943 to provide tactical air support to the ground forces that were soon to land in France. During the following six months, the strength of the 9th was built up with the Republic Thunderbolt becoming its main fighter type. One fighter group of the 9th, the 366th, assembled at Membury after crossing from America. The three squadrons, 389th, 390th and 391st, flew their Thunderbolts from Membury in a working up capacity before moving to Thruxton. Their departure allowed the 436th Troop Carrier Group to move in from Bottesford on 3rd March 1944.

Under the command of Colonel Adriel N. Williams, the 436th was formed in 1943 in the USA and was made up of sheet metal workers, motor mechanics and many more trades. Consisting of the 79th, 80th, 81st and 82nd Troop Carrier Squadrons, the group flew the C-47 to be used in conjunction with the airborne forces. Many of the aircraft were flown directly to Bottesford whilst the majority of the men were transported by the *Queen Mary* to Liverpool and thence to Bottesford. Training began immediately in parachute dropping and glider towing by day and by night. The 436th then participated in four major airborne operations before renewing a period of intense training, this being carried out incorporating the 101st Airborne, known to all as the 'Screaming Eagles'! Although still a secret, the training was in preparation for D-Day. On the eve of the greatest invasion of the war, Air Marshal Sir

Crest of the 436th Troop Carrier Group, Membury. (C Samson)

Trafford Leigh-Mallory visited Membury and spoke words of encouragement to all the men participating in the assault.

Postponed for 24 hours, the invasion went ahead in the early hours of 6th June. With Membury a hive of activity and the entire area reverberating to the sound of the Pratt and Whitney engines of the C-47s, the first operation was 'Albany', the Normandy airlift, which involved 90 aircraft carrying 1,084 paratroops of the US 101st Airborne Division. They were dropped in and around the Normandy town of Ste Mere-Eglise, but 'Albany' was only partially successful, as many of the troops were dropped off the target. The 436th were later tasked in the second glider airlift for the 82nd Airborne, using two Hadrians and 48 Horsas to carry the 377th Parachute Field Artillery Regiment. The Allied forces were well and truly ashore and pushing hard inland.

History records the success of 'Operation Overlord' and for its good work over the 6th and 7th of June, the 436th received a Distinguished Unit Citation. D-Day was an operation which was led by three airborne divisions, followed by five assault divisions with tanks landing on the beaches, followed by six more divisions with 21 more waiting in England. They were carried by 4,262 aircraft and 4,266 ships of all kinds and supported by 2,300 combat aircraft which flew 14,600 sorties on D-Day alone. In all of

Sir Trafford Leigh-Mallory, General Eisenhower's Air Commander for D-Day, addressing men of the 436th TCG from the Membury control tower (his hands on the rail), 4th June 1944. (Ian McLoughlin)

this, Membury had played a crucial part. With the Allied armies advancing quickly into France, the 436th continued the airlift of supplies, joined on D-Day+1 by the aircraft of the 442nd TCG.

With 'Overlord' over, thoughts turned to the next phase in the push to victory. During July, a detachment of C-47s from the 436th TCG flew to Italy to take part in 'Operation Anvil', the amphibious invasion of southern France. It was however the next operation, 'Market Garden' that prompted further men to be shipped over from the USA to join the 436th TCG at Membury.

The film *A Bridge Too Far*, which depicts the story of the operation, has become a movie classic. Sticking roughly to the true story of what happened, it tells the tale of blunder and tragedy. Like the Normandy operation that preceded it, it is now part of British and American history that is debated still today. Although the Allies had made headway into France from the Normandy invasion, they were unable to push on through Holland into Germany. The appalling weather and the fact that fuel and ammunition for the

35

Airborne troops practise for the invasion – such scenes became commonplace during 1943 and 1944. (SE Newspapers)

advancing Allies had to come through Normandy were limiting the speed at which the advance could continue.

As 17th September 1944 approached, a cloak of security was thrown around Membury. As we have seen at the beginning of the chapter, 'Market Garden' was not the success that D-Day proved. For Membury, the two flights of 45 C-47s met far more intense flak than during the Normandy landings. During the dropping of the paratroops of the 101st, five aircraft were lost with a further 13 damaged during the first sortie. For the second drop, 11 aircraft were damaged. The following day, the C-47s and the gliders were airborne again over Holland, this time losing one with two further aircraft crash-landing back at Membury. On the third day, bad weather seriously disrupted the tows, but the sorties that were flown incurred several losses of aircraft. On 20th September, 80 C-47s dropped supplies to the troops below whilst on the 23rd, 46 aircraft towed gliders to the battle area with reinforcements. By the evening of the 23rd, no further sorties were flown in support of the landings and Membury once again became a little quieter.

The winter of 1944/5 saw the 436th transporting further supplies to the Continent and carrying on the ever important training and exercises. As the new year of 1945 dawned, an air of expectancy pervaded the entire base. On 1st January, the Luftwaffe employed over 800 aircraft to attack Allied airfields in France, Belgium and Holland. It proved a disaster for the enemy and was the last major attack by the Luftwaffe. Despite this resurgence, everyone knew that time was running out for the enemy. By February, the British and Canadians had broken through the Siegfried Line and had reached the Rhine. Although the 436th had carried out supply drops over this period, the time had come for the unit to move into France and nearer the action. Between the 21st and 25th February 1945, they moved onto the Continent to be based at Melun (A-55). The 436th TCG finally returned to the United States in August 1945 and were later inactivated.

As the Americans left, Membury was handed back to the RAF. The plan was to be ready on 1st July and to be taken over by No 47 Group, Transport Command, but it was not until the 15th of the month that the Dakotas of No 525 Squadron moved in from

Planes and gliders lined up at Membury ready for take-off – XVIII Corps, 14th November 1944. (Signal Corps)

nearby Lyneham. They were joined by No 187 Squadron from Merryfield in October. Also flying Dakotas, both squadrons were tasked with carrying troops to the Far East. This continued for a year but with the advent of larger four-engined aircraft, the Dakotas were reduced to continental mail and newspaper deliveries. This continued until October 1946 when they moved to new locations and Membury was placed under Care and Maintenance, parented by Welford.

The base was considered as a possible Strategic Air Command airfield but with various problems arising, Greenham Common was chosen instead. A resurgence of use came in 1966 when the Campbell Aircraft Company of Hungerford used Membury for flight testing their gyrocopters. Testing and production continued until the company closed down in 1976.

Today, part of the airfield is the M4 motorway, complete with a service station. Many of the buildings remain, now used by light industry, whilst the T2 hangars are used for storing grain and hay. One of the local companies uses the control tower as an office and has placed plaques in memory of both American and British servicemen who had served at Membury around the walls, a fitting tribute indeed. On the 54th anniversary of 'Market Garden', 17th September 1998, a unique gathering of veterans and American and British serving personnel took place. Connected to the opening of the new Jacquet Weston plant on the airfield site, it rekindled many memories of those troop-carrying days of 1944/5.

5

WELFORD

When the wartime programme for airfield requirements was drawn up in August 1940, it was proposed to site the majority of bomber OTUs in the Midlands. Over the course of further planning, some came into the Berkshire region. It was further suggested that bomber OTUs should have a second satellite and that a total of 43 OTUs would be necessary in the UK. This was enough to equip the RAF whilst any surplus airfields went to the USAAF. One of these surplus airfields was Welford.

Situated seven miles north-west of Newbury, the airfield was built on a flat area of land close to the River Lambourn. Authorised in October 1941 as an OTU, building commenced immediately after the land had been requisitioned from local landowners. It was built to a standard bomber airfield pattern with a three runway layout, the main one of 2,000 feet being aligned north-west/south-east. Two T-Type hangars were built together with a total of 50 aircraft hardstandings consisting of 46 loops and four pans. Accommodation and technical sites were situated within the airfield boundary as the thinking was that Welford, so far from the area of enemy action, would not be of interest to the Luftwaffe. It had already been earmarked for No 92 Group, Bomber Command and was also classified as a second satellite to Membury.

Taking until 21st April 1943 to be completed, it was No 70 Group RAF that accepted responsibility for RAF Welford. By 10th

June the forward party had arrived to set up the SHQ but already Welford had been allocated to the USAAF. This became official in July and by 6th September 1943, the Americans had arrived and Welford became US Station 474 (Welford Park).

Once again, as with all the bomber OTUs handed over to the USAAF within the area, the base was to become a Troop Carrier Wing. Nothing happened until November when the remnants of the 315th TCG arrived from nearby Aldermaston. Welford Park came to near full capacity one month later when the 434th TCG (71st, 72nd, 73rd and 74th TCS) arrived from Fulbeck. Flying C-47s, they began an intensive training period with gliders and troops.

They returned to Fulbeck after a short stay and were replaced by the 435th TCG (75th, 76th, 77th and 78th TCS). Commanded by Colonel Frank J. MacNees, the 435th also commenced a period of training. They were joined by the 438th TCG (87th, 88th, 89th and 90th TCS) later in the month, also flying C-47s. Welford Park suddenly seemed very crowded with personnel and aircraft. With little rest from training over the festive period, both units transferred to the 9th Air Force on 22nd February 1944. The 438th moved over to Greenham Common on 16th March leaving Welford Park to the 435th TCG and the US 101st Airborne Division.

Crest of the 435th Troop Carrier Group, Welford Park. (C Samson)

With the planning for 'Overlord' at an advanced stage, the C-47s and C-53 transport aircraft began practice tows with US Waco CG-4A and British Airspeed Horsa gliders. It was with the success of the German airborne forces sweeping through Norway, Belgium and Holland during the summer of 1940, that the training of airborne forces in Britain had been given a priority. The use of gliders for carrying troops started when the Central Landing School was formed at Ringway, Manchester. Later the gliding training section was split

A Horsa glider of the 101st Airborne Division lands at dawn on a field at Welford, 12th May 1944. (Signal Corps)

off to become No 1 Glider Training School at RAF Croughton in Northamptonshire.

Between 1940 and 1945, over 1,000 training gliders and over 4,000 operational gliders were produced in Britain for the RAF. Others were supplied by the Americans, with the first British airborne operations with gliders (over Norway) taking place on 19th November 1942 and the last (across the Rhine) in March 1945. Of the two types of gliders used in the training and eventual assault on France, the Horsa had a crew of two and should carry 20 to 25 troops. The other type used in the assault was the American Waco Hadrian glider, which was considerably smaller. First supplied to the RAF in 1943, they were used in the Allied invasion of Sicily in July 1943. This was their only use in RAF operations, but the Americans continued to use them for 'Overlord' and for the intensive training programme at Welford Park and other bases.

As the rehearsal for the assault gathered pace, Welford Park played host to Mr Churchill and General Eisenhower. They arrived when 97 gliders were being towed off on a formation, cross-country exercise. After release at a designated place, they all returned to the airfield precisely on time, a perfect demonstration of just how efficient the carriers and the airborne forces had become.

As 6th June approached, an intense security cordon was thrown around Welford Park. Shortly after midnight on 5th June, the familiar drone of hundreds of aircraft engines above the south coast of England caused people to lift the black-out curtains of their

Part of the vast Allied airborne army which participated in the invasion of Holland, preparing to board their transport planes, 1944. (National Archives)

rooms and peer up at the sky. For months, the noise of engines had been heard departing and returning. However, on this particular night, the sound was more intense and did not return until much later than usual. 'Operation Overlord' had begun.

As dawn approached on the 6th, the 435th left Welford Park to carry out the first wave of paratroop drops. Men of the 101st Airborne Divisional Headquarters, including the Divisional Commander, Major General Maxwell D. Taylor, together with the 2nd Battalion 501st Parachute Infantry Regiment were dropped at designated zones near Cherbourg. Cloud cover over the beaches caused a few problems but the drop in the main was successful. Three C-47s and their gliders were lost to enemy action with seven more damaged. These were able to land back at base and after being repaired, were sent once again to tow more gliders and troops. The towing operations continued throughout the next day but with airstrips on the Continent now rapidly becoming available to the Allies, the despatching of medical supplies, food and ammunition became the priority. Landing at the hastily made strips, the C-47s brought back the wounded to Welford Park who were then taken to hospitals in the Newbury area.

A BBC war correspondent gives us the flavour of the operation in his own words:

'From where I am, standing between the two pilots of this glider, I can see the navigation lights of the tug in front of us and off to the left and right, the navigation lights of other tugs and other gliders bound on the same mission. Circling above from time to time, I can see the lights of the fighter screen which is protecting us. And looking back down the glider, there are seated, although I can hardly see them in the half light, officers and men all laden with equipment so heavy that they can barely walk. They have to carry with them items with which they can fight the moment they land. We are over the enemy coast now and the run-in has started. One minute. Thirty seconds. Red light. Green light. Out, out. Get out! Out into the cool night. Out into the area over France but we know the dropping zone is obstructed. We are in fact jumping into fields that are covered in poles. But I hit my chute and lower my kit bag

46

The sky was filled with paratroops as D-Day drew near. (SE Newspapers)

which is suspended on the end of a 40 foot rope from my harness. And then the ground comes up to hit me and I find myself in the middle of a cornfield. Suddenly all hell is let loose as the enemy realise what is happening. There is firing all around us and we throw ourselves to the ground. This is D-Day in France.'

The words of General Eisenhower, the Supreme Commander of the Allied Forces, did however bring a ray of hope to the oppressed:

'People of Western Europe. A landing was made this morning on the coast of France by troops of the Allied Expeditionary Force. This landing is a part of a united nations plan for the liberation of Europe, made in conjunction with our great Russian allies. I have this message for all of you. Although the initial assault may not have been made in your own country, the hour of your liberation is approaching.'

The foothold in Europe had been gained and Welford Park had played an important role in its success. For its part in 'Overlord', the 435th received a Distinguished Unit Citation. There was, however, no rest for the 435th TCG as a detachment was sent to Italy to participate in Operation Anvil, the amphibious assault on southern France. The aircraft remained until the end of August when they flew back to Welford Park and into another period of intensive training.

The remainder of the unit began transport services following the landings and intermittently were engaged in missions of that type until VE Day. In addition they delivered supplies such as serum, blood plasma, radar sets, clothing, rations and ammunition before evacuating wounded personnel to Allied hospitals. For the 435th and the 101st Airborne, the next operation was 'Market Garden', the ill-fated invasion to capture vital river bridges in Holland.

'Market Garden' began in the early hours of 17th September 1944 and just after 10 am on the same day, 36 C-47s were rolling down the runway of Welford Park towing gliders containing paratroops of the 101st Airborne to drop just north of the Wilhelmina Canal near Eindhoven. The routes were marked by beacons and coded lights on Channel shipping. Full air cover was provided by around 1,000 British and American fighters although the greatest danger came from flak. The sheer ferocity of this brought down two C-47s and damaged ten more in the first sortie whilst another eight were damaged in the second.

Over the drop zone, the C-47s released their gliders which landed very accurately. Gathering together their fire-power, the 101st very soon captured the two southern bridges between Veghel and Eindhoven. This initial success, however, was not to be applied to the other forces who met heavy resistance as soon as they landed. Whilst history records that 'Market Garden' was not a total failure due to the securing of two passages across the Maas and Waal Canals, many good lives were lost and their sacrifice marked the end of any hopes of ending the war in 1944.

As the C-47s returned to Welford Park, some badly damaged, thoughts turned to those who would not be coming back. The next two days saw further glider tows together with supply drops. 'Market Garden' finally closed on 25th September with the

48

Preparation for an aerial resupply exercise for American troops of the 101st AD. (Signal Corps)

evacuation of the surviving paratroops. There was, however, no slowing of the pace as during mid December, the enemy launched a major offensive through the Ardennes in eastern Belgium. With the 101st Airborne encircling the town of Bastogne, the C-47s from Welford Park and other bases kept up the job of resupplying them until they were able to be relieved.

As 1945 dawned, the 435th prepared to move to Bretigny in France. After a very successful time at Welford Park and with victory in sight at last, the fight was being carried back to the Continent. The 435th moved back to the United States in August 1945 and were in-activated on 15th November before being placed on the reserve list. After many years as a base of the USAAF, Welford Park was returned to the RAF in June 1945 and reverted to its original name of Welford.

Taken over by Transport Command, No 1336 (Transport Support) Conversion Unit was formed at Welford on 30th June 1945. Courses began in August with Dakotas and Horsas, these continuing until 1st March 1946 when the unit was cut. Welford was then reduced to Care and Maintenance for a short period before transferring to No 90 (Signals) Group in October 1946. The association with flying did not entirely stop at this point thanks to the enterprise of a local company. Elliots of Newbury had designed and built the Eon, a four-seat light aeroplane, during 1946/7. Looking for a site from which to test-fly it, they approached the Air Ministry with a view to using Welford. With permission granted, they commenced flight trials in August 1947. The company was joined by the headquarters of the Southern Signals Areas which had formed at Welford at the same time. Both Elliots and the headquarters stayed for around two years despite the transfer of the airfield from a signals group to Maintenance Command in 1950. Reduced to Care and Maintenance once again on 1st August 1952, it was to remain this way for two years.

New life was breathed into the airfield in 1955 when it was accepted, once again, as a logistics base for the USAAF. With an intense security cordon being installed around Welford and the construction of storage bunkers, a munitions depot took over the entire site. It became the main ammunition dump for all the American bases in the UK and remained that way administered by the 100th Regional Support Group for the 20th Fighter Wing of the 3rd Air Force until it disbanded. It gave valuable support to NATO throughout the 'Cold War' period and in 1991, the base and personnel of the 850th Munitions Maintenance Squadron USAF, along with British service and civilian staff, made a significant contribution to the Allied victory in the first Gulf War. On 1st April 1995, RAF Welford became a joint-use facility operated by the USAF 424th Air Base Squadron and the Royal Air Force until 1999, when the base was transferred to the MOD Defence Munitions Agency. In November 2002, RAF Welford was again back in USAF hands being the full responsibility of the 424th Air Base Squadron at RAF Fairford. The base remains one of the largest munitions stores for the USAF in Europe.

A significant amount of its World War II configuration remains, the T-2 Hangars are still in use, as well as many wartime buildings, including several nissen huts.

In remembrance of all the units that served at Welford, a memorial was erected in 1993 close to the entrance.

6

WHITE WALTHAM

Now operated by the West London Aero Club, White Waltham was built between the wars on 196 acres of grassland purchased by the de Havilland family to house the de Havilland School of Flying. Lying two miles south-west of Maidenhead, it is a grass airfield that is reportedly the largest in the country.

With the purchase and setting up of the flying school in 1928, a succession of pupils passed through the school until, with signs of another war with Germany, it was taken over by the government to become the home of No. 13 Elementary and Reserve Flying Training School, on 18th November, 1935. The pupils, all volunteers, had to be educated to School Certificate standard and be between the ages of 18 and 25. After swearing in, they were given the complimentary rank of Sergeant with obligations to report immediately if and when war broke out, to attend training regularly and to fly whenever instructed. For this they were to be paid the sum of 10 shillings each day during training and 12 shillings and sixpence when qualified as a pilot. By 3rd September, 1939 when war finally broke out, the unit was renamed No. 13 Elementary Flying Training School with relief landing grounds (RLGs) at Henley and Bray. Flying the venerable Tiger Moth the school remained at White Waltham until December 1940, when it moved to Westwood near Peterborough.

The Faithful Annie – an Avro Anson used to transport ATA pilots at White Waltham airfield. (MAP)

It was after this that the airfield entered the most famous period of its existence when it became the home of the newly formed Air Transport Auxiliary. This was the organisation tasked with delivering aircraft direct from the factories to the airfields and squadrons of the various commands. It began as No. 3 Ferry Pilots Pool which was formed on 15th February, 1940 with nine aircraft and forty pilots. Initially, they were only allowed to fly aircraft such as the Tiger Moth and later Miles Magisters, but the exigencies of war soon demanded that this was extended to almost all military aircraft. Many flyers came from overseas to join the organisation and having travelled by sea from their countries, the last piece of the jigsaw was a train journey from Paddington to White Waltham where they would find the usual RAF collection of Nissen huts which was to become their home for some considerable time. It was cold and miserable and, with a grass airfield, the mud seemed to be everywhere. White Waltham, however, bathed in the glow of being the headquarters of the ATA with several 'pools' scattered around various airfields of the UK. It was here that a list of all the aircraft to be moved on any particular day would be promulgated and issued to the other pools accordingly. It could be a Tiger Moth, Spitfire, Hurricane, Barracuda or any of the four-engined bombers; all of these came within the responsibility of the ATA.

The airfield was to remain the headquarters of the organisation until 30th November 1945, when the ATA was disbanded. One month earlier, an Air Display and Air Pageant was opened by Lord Beaverbrook and included a static display of allied aircraft, with a display by Alex Henshaw flying a Seafire Mark 45. Despite being threatened with closure, White Waltham survived and was used by Fairey Aviation and Westland Helicopters during the post-war years. In 1952, Prince Philip, Duke of Edinburgh, learnt to fly in a Chipmunk of the Communications Squadron when the airfield was taken over by the RAF to the headquarters of RAF Home Command. This lasted until 1982, when the MOD relinquished the airfield and it was purchased by the current owners.

Today, White Waltham is a very busy airfield but remains a grass one with three runways still in situ. From the de Havilland days through to war and back to peace, the airfield has come full circle.

7

THE AIR TRANSPORT AUXILIARY

At a disbanding ceremony held on 30th November 1945 at White Waltham airfield, Lord Beaverbrook paid tribute to the ATA in his speech: 'Without the ATA the days and nights of the Battle of Britain would have been conducted under conditions quite different from the actual events. They carried out the delivery of aircraft from the factories to the RAF thus relieving countless numbers of RAF pilots for duty in the battle. Just as the Battle of Britain is the accomplishment and achievement of the RAF, likewise it can be declared that the ATA sustained and supported them in the battle. They were soldiers fighting in the struggle just as completely as if they had been engaged on front-line duties.'

Fine words for a job well done but also for an organisation that is still waiting for its own individual medal today. The ATA was originally intended to be a civilian-run unit solely employed to transport people and medical supplies. Gerard d'Erlanger, a director of British Overseas Airways Corporation (BOAC), had suggested a similar type of organisation before the war. His own foresight told him that another conflict was imminent and that civilian pilots such as himself could help the war effort. A letter written by him on 24th May 1938 to the Air Ministry stated that such pilots who did not meet military standards, either on age or fitness, could be employed on ferrying aircraft. Initially, his idea was not taken up.

The outbreak of war, however, did bring an official change of heart and in August 1939, the RAF Ferry Pools (as they were initially known) began transporting military aircraft from the factories to the maintenance units and airfields. The organization initially only recruited male pilots from BOAC, who also controlled administration and finance. A month after the war began the Air Member for Supply and Organisation (AMSO) took over control from BOAC, with the pilots being assigned to the RAF Reserve Command. However, with the country desperately short of combat pilots, some were taken from the ferry pools and this opened the way for female pilots to join.

By early 1940 a ferry pool had been set up at White Waltham aerodrome. With the organisation now officially known as the Air Transport Auxiliary, it fell to Commander Pauline Gower to manage the women's section. In May 1940, the entire ferry organisation moved under the control of RAF Maintenance Command, then to the Ministry of Aircraft Production (MAP) in July 1941.

Overall administration remained firmly in the hands of BOAC and Commander Gerard d' Erlanger. Under him, an intense programme of flying training began for the many female volunteers. They came from all over the Commonwealth, the USA, Netherlands, Poland and a sole lady from Argentina, Maureen Dunlop. A wartime issue of *Picture Post* featured Maureen on its front cover. The first rule dictated that the women were restricted to trainers and transport aircraft. This however soon changed when it was realised that they were as skilled as their male counterparts. It was perhaps also the first time that equality between the sexes prevailed when it was agreed that they should get the same pay as the male pilots.

Initial training was at the RAF Central Flying School but this changed when the ATA took over the airfield at White Waltham and developed their own training programme. With the same criteria for pilot selection as the males, the recruitment form stated that the ATA would consider all pilots who were unsuitable for full military flying for reasons of age or fitness. Physical handicaps were ignored if the pilot could do the job. Thus if you only had one arm or leg, were short-sighted or had just one eye, if you could fly an aeroplane you were in! One of the women recruited to this organisation was First Officer Mary Wilkins who now lives quietly on the Isle of Wight:

'When I saw the advertisement for women pilots I thought that must be fun. I could not even drive a car but I had learnt to fly at Witney airfield so I went along to the interview. I am a very tiny lady and I wondered if my height and physical appearance would jeopardise my chances. However it did not because the officer interviewing said, "Oh well, you can always sit on a cushion." Which was exactly what I had to do to see over the dash!

'Once I had been accepted I went on an extensive training course and from that time on I never looked back. And really on reflection it was the time of my life. I learnt not only flying but navigation, map reading etc all of which was carried out in the air with an instructor.

'We started flying Moths and Magisters, Harts and Hinds and the lovely Avro Tutor. We had no radio or any other navigational aids, just relying on maps, the compass and the watch.

'Oh, it was so exciting in those first few months even if it was very cold in the open cockpit of a Tiger Moth. You needed a helmet, I had a white leather one and an Irvin leather flying jacket. We were issued with lovely leather and canvas boots, up to the knee and of

First Officer Mary Wilkins ATA.

course goggles. However, it was also known that occasionally we flew with just a headscarf (though this was against regulations).

'In January 1942 my female group was posted to White Waltham where we carried on with further navigational training and got to fly a Harvard. That was a superior aircraft to the Moths and Magisters and was the next step down from flying a Spitfire.

'From White Waltham I flew Hurricanes, Spitfires, Lysanders, Defiants, Mustangs and Typhoons. By October 1942 I was flying Wellingtons, Mitchells and other twin-engined aircraft. However, I also flew my first Spitfire from here and this began a love affair with that particular aircraft. My first flight in one was from South Marston to Lyneham. As I was strapping myself in, with the help of an engineer, he asked me, "Hope you enjoy your flight, how many have you flown?" He was horrified, poor man, when I replied, "Oh, this is my first." I am sure my little heart was beating fast as I taxied down and lined up for take-off knowing that all the engineers were watching. I made an excellent job of it however and went on to fly many Spitfires of different marks. I was also the first and only ATA pilot to deliver the jet-engined Meteor.'

As D-Day drew near, the airfield and the ATA in general became increasingly busy. On D-Day itself, Mary Wilkins delivered two Spitfires and a Fairchild Argus. One Spitfire was flown from Hamble to Cowley, the second from Hamble to Aston Down and a Fairchild from Brize Norton to Hamble. In order to get them to the point of pick-up, the ATA operated an air taxi service with aircraft such as Fairchild Argus or, for more capacity, the Avro Anson known to all as 'Faithful Annie'. These aircraft were constantly flying between the various ferry pools, often in difficult weather conditions. In the run up to D-Day, it was imperative that new aircraft and repaired aircraft were flown to the squadrons as quickly as possible. Thus, the taxi service was constantly flying the pilots from first light to dusk.

'What was my least favourite aircraft? The Supermarine Walrus. This single-engined pusher prop aircraft was so slow and sluggish that some of the girls used to take their sewing with them and

57

Page from the pilot's log book of First Officer Mary Wilkins ATA which includes 6th June 1944 – D-Day.

attempt to work on darning whilst flying. However, the aircraft did sterling work in air-sea rescue and saved many airmen from drowning.

'My favourite? Need you ask? The Spitfire. It was a magnificent aircraft and luckily I got to fly in one recently when I got a ride in the Grace Spitfire. When the ATA disbanded I know all the girls were so sad. We all missed it terribly. Luckily I was able to carry on in aviation and became the managing director of Sandown Airport on the Isle of Wight. I now live very close to it still and whenever I hear a Merlin engine, I am out in the garden and looking up together with all the memories that go with that sound.'

There were many more brave female pilots. It is not within the confines of this chapter to name them all, but one that has always fired the public imagination as to what did happen when she disappeared without trace, was Amy Johnson CBE.

Sunday, 5th January 1941, was a drab and melancholy day, not a good day for flying. Amy Johnson was detailed to fly a twin-engined Oxford from Squires Gate airfield near Blackpool to Kidlington airfield near Oxford that day, but the persistent drizzle and low cloud had hampered an early morning take-off. With the promise of an improvement during the afternoon she prepared to leave Squires Gate, finally lifting off at 11.49 am. The aircraft that the ATA flew had no navigational aids or radio, they flew with just a compass and map. Flights depended upon seeing the ground, but on this occasion it would have been difficult for Amy to compare the ground with her map. She never did arrive at Kidlington and since that time there have been various explanations as to what happened. The most likely is that she went a long way off course, finally running out of petrol whilst in the region of the Thames estuary. Sometime after she was reported missing the crew of a destroyer, HMS *Haslemere*, stated that they heard an aircraft in cloud pass over them as they were sailing up the Thames estuary. Looking up they saw a parachute descending and finally hitting the icy cold water. Attempting to close on the parachute, the Commanding Officer, Lt Cmdr Walter Fletcher, jumped into the sea and swam towards the floating object. Sadly, the cold and the tide overcame him and he died in the attempt to rescue Amy, who herself was swept away and presumably drowned. She was the first ATA female pilot to die in service, though others were to follow as the war continued.

It was a sad Friday when at around 4.30 pm the ATA flag was lowered at White Waltham. As a final tribute, a single Avro Anson landed and dispatched a few men from the organisation to join the women. No finer tribute could have been paid to them all than the words spoken by Lord Beaverbrook. The Air Transport Auxiliary were indeed, 'fine soldiers in the front line of duty.'

Mary Ellis (née Wilkins), with the author, at her home on the Isle of Wight.

8

WOODLEY

It was on the outbreak of war that the existing network of Elementary & Reserve Flying Training Schools (E&RFTS) was reorganised. Many schools were closed or amalgamated to form a new training system. These became known as the Elementary Flying Training Schools. One of the larger schools was formed on 3rd September 1939, the day that war broke out. This was No 8 EFTS, at Woodley near Reading.

A rather small grass airfield, since the mid 1930s it had trained 680 pilots and 108 navigators. The Order of Battle for the RAF in January 1939 stated that Woodley was an airfield in Training Command with its headquarters at Market Drayton in Shropshire. It was also the base for the Reading Royal Air Force Volunteer Reserve whose pilots were trained by the former E&RFTS. Commanded by Wing Commander L.I. Griffiths, the pilots were given initial training at Woodley before progressing to the Flying Training Schools. Though not a fighter station, Woodley was allocated a decoy airfield which was situated at Warfield. It never served its intended purpose for Woodley was not on the enemy hit list. Once the Battle of Britain was over, the decoy was derequisitioned.

In addition to the EFTS, Miles Aircraft Ltd had established a factory at Woodley before the war. One of their most famous designs and one that served at many of the flying training schools, was the Magister. Known to thousands of RAF pilots who learnt to fly on the type as 'the Maggie', it was the first monoplane trainer to be used by the RAF. First delivered to the service in October 1937, it was an all-wooden aircraft derived from the earlier well known series of civil aircraft produced by Mr E.G. Miles and known as the 'Hawks'. Beginning with the Cirrus Hawk of 1932, it included such types as the Hawk Major, Hawk Speed Six and Hawk Trainer. As they rolled out of the Woodley factory, No 8 EFTS became one of the first schools to be equipped with Hawk trainers. Production of the Magister ended in 1941 after 1,203 aircraft had been built, many of them going to the flying training schools such as No 8 at Woodley.

Later designs from the Miles stable were the Miles Master Trainer, first delivered in May 1939 but not nearly as successful as the Magister, and the Miles Martinet, designed as a target tug. In 1943, Miles Aircraft began work on a radio-controlled pilotless version of the Martinet. The original version was superseded by the Queen Martinet which reached a production total of 65. All of these aircraft were built, tested and flown from Woodley making it a very important manufacturing airfield. Long before this however, Woodley had witnessed an accident that would change the life of one man and create a Second World War legend.

The basic fighter trainer of 1938/9, made at Woodley airfield – the Miles Magister. (L Pilkington)

Monday, 14th December 1931 dawned clear and fine. At RAF Kenley, nestling high on the hills above Caterham in Surrey, the Bristol Bulldogs of No 23 Squadron were lined up in the dispersal area, the early morning sun glinting on their polished aluminium. Two pilots of the squadron, Phillips and Richardson, had arranged to fly to Woodley Aerodrome to see a relation who ran the flying club. They were joined by a third man, Pilot Officer Douglas Bader, who suggested that he tag along for the ride. Getting airborne, it did not take long to reach Woodley and all three aircraft landed and taxied up to the clubhouse for coffee and biscuits. Very soon, Bader was engaged in conversation with some of the flying club members who were asking about aerobatics. It was later suggested that he give the flying club a demonstration, but Bader gracefully declined, acting on the orders of his commanding officer back at Kenley, Surrey. Pilots were forbidden to practise unauthorised aerobatics below 2,000 feet. It was just a mild comment of 'windy' from one of the club members that made him change his mind with all the eventual consequences. Bader had a reputation for being a daredevil.

Richardson took off first followed by Bader. It was the latter who went directly into an aerobatic routine, flying almost at ground level as he swooped over the clubhouse. It was during one particular manoeuvre that entailed rolling upside down that he felt his aircraft dropping. Attempting to straighten up, his wingtip hit the grass and pulled the Bulldog down to earth. The aircraft crumpled as the engine was torn out of the fuselage. It careered across the grass before coming to a stop.

Bader could feel nothing as his straps continued to hold him tightly in the cockpit. Suddenly all was quiet as he drifted in and out of consciousness. The members of the flying club rushed to help him out as smoke began to come from the crumpled fuselage. As the ambulance arrived, Bader was lifted onto a stretcher and taken to hospital, where he had to come to terms with the loss of both legs. The rest of Douglas Bader's life is a legend and an inspiration on how to overcome a disability.

The training of pilots continued uninterrupted until 20th July 1942 when No 10 Flying Instructors School took over from No 8 EFTS. Some of the Miles Magisters were exchanged for the venerable Tiger Moth. From this time until the end of the war, training continued apace at Woodley, the amount of flying training giving cause to use Henley as a Relief Landing Ground.

With the war over, Woodley quickly became surplus to RAF requirements and from a busy wartime airfield producing and test-flying Miles aircraft, training pilots and repairing damaged aircraft such as Spitfires, it became a part-time base. No 10 FIS survived until 1st June 1945 when it was disbanded.

A few Tiger Moths remained and with these, No 8 EFTS was reformed on 7th May 1946. It had been felt by the Air Ministry that wartime pilots who wanted to continue flying, could join the RAF Volunteer Reserve and continue to fly and train at the EFTS. No 8 was instantly retitled No 8 Reserve Flying School. It was equipped with twelve Tiger Moths and two Anson T1s, these being used mainly for refresher flying. The schools were joined by the Flying Training Command Communications Flight from 1946 until 1951 using a variety of aircraft such as Ansons, Harvards and a Dakota, the personal mount of the C-in-C, Training Command.

Woodley now settled into a peacetime routine. The Tiger Moths were replaced with Chipmunks in 1951, but their use was shortlived as in January 1953 it was announced that seven of the 20 Reserve Flying Schools were to close. Sadly, No 8 RFS was one and it duly disbanded on 31st March 1955. It was the death knell for Woodley for, with Miles Aircraft Ltd ceasing production, all flying stopped. The site fell into disrepair only to be built upon in later years. The airfield had served the nation well, with many aircrew gaining their first introduction to flight at Woodley.

A fine shot of Woodley, the Miles Aircraft Factory and the Miles M.18 prototype. Note the camouflaged hangars. (Crown via B Robertson)

9
THE SMALLER
BERKSHIRE AIRFIELDS

Winkfield

Though just a Relief Landing Ground for the Tiger Moths of No 18 EFTS based at Fairoaks, Winkfield served in this capacity from 28th May 1941 until 9th July 1945. It had very few facilities, was just a small grass airfield and saw very little use. Immediately after the war it was de-requisitioned, and today is the site of a radio and space research establishment.

Smith's Lawn

A private landing strip during the 1930s, Smith's Lawn in the south-east corner of Windsor Great Park, was selected as a possible site for an airfield. Vickers Armstrong arrived during 1940 and erected a Bellman hangar, eventually starting a production line known as VAXI (Vickers Armstrong Extension 1). Production began of the Wellington Mks V and VI, special high altitude versions of the twin-engined bomber. In addition, the airfield was an RLG for the Tiger Moths of No 18 EFTS based at Fairoaks in Surrey.

The NAAFI wagon – whatever the size of airfield you were based on, this was a welcome sight!

Production of the Wellingtons at Smith's Lawn totalled 65 before the end of the war halted all further building. A quantity of Vickers Warwick bombers were stored at the airfield and it was also used by an American unit until 1946. Reverting back to its park status in 1947, it is nowadays better known for its sporting activities.

Theale

There is no doubt that the world's most famous training aircraft is the de Havilland Tiger Moth. It remained in service with the RAF for over 15 years and many of them are still flying today in civilian hands. The last biplane trainer in the RAF, it was still being used as a standard elementary trainer as late as 1947 in Flying Training Command and until 1951 with the RAF Volunteer Reserve.

Derived from the Gipsy Moth range of pre-war club aircraft, it differed from the type in having staggered and swept-back wings, this to enable an easier parachute escape from the front cockpit. Ordered by the Air Ministry to Spec.23/31, the prototype first flew on 26th October 1931. By the outbreak of war, over 1,000 Tiger Moths had been delivered, most of them serving with the Elementary and Reserve Flying Training Schools where RAF pilots were given initial instruction before proceeding to the service flying training schools. The other Air Ministry *ab initio* training organisations to use the Tiger Moth were the Elementary Flying Training Schools. Theale supported one of these schools for the duration of the war.

Situated some three miles west of Reading and bounded by the Kennet and Avon Canal to the north, the field was requisitioned by the Air Ministry in 1940. Initially it had been known as Sheffield Farm and was classed as a Relief Landing Ground to nearby Woodley airfield. It had a rough surface and it was therefore necessary to sow new grass. This took some time before the Ministry found it acceptable. When they did, they authorised the formation of an Elementary Flying Training School to be run under contract by Phillips and Powis Aircraft Ltd. The airfield officially opened on 14th August 1941 and was immediately renamed Theale. It was however, far from complete and a period of heavy rainfall had shown up a considerable water-logging problem.

Two Blister hangars had been erected together with several brick buildings for use as stores or classrooms, but very little airmen's accommodation had been completed. Despite these obvious problems, No 26 EFTS formed at Theale on 21st July 1941 with a complement of 24 Tiger Moths and 60 pupils. The instructors had been posted in from No 8 EFTS but the majority of ground services were handled by civilian personnel under the control of No 50 Group of the RAF. With no buildings complete, the pupils were accommodated in a large country house about a mile from the airfield. Sulhamstead House had been requisitioned for this purpose and was also to act as a school for navigation instruction etc.

The first flying course commenced on 21st August 1941, with the last one finishing on 30th June 1945. The venerable Tiger

Moth remained the main type flown but various other types used Theale for communication purposes. Night flying was carried out at White Waltham, there being no facilities at Theale for this type of training. Being an EFTS, there were several major incidents but in the main, Theale had a good safety record.

No 26 EFTS were joined by No 128 Gliding School during 1944. Formed to give Air Cadets experience in gliding, the Slingsby Cadet gliders became as familiar as the Tiger Moths around the local area.

With the end of the war, No 26 EFTS became one of the first to close down. All flying ceased on 30th June 1945. Theale was quickly reduced to Care and Maintenance although 28 Tiger Moths were left sitting around the airfield perimeter awaiting dispersal. The Air Cadets continued to use the facilities until 1948 when the airfield was de-requisitioned and left to an unknown fate. It did not have to wait long before a gravel company moved in and the majority of the site became an enormous pit. The pits are now flooded and used for watersports. Some buildings, including the T1 hangar survived, but the rest have sadly disappeared for ever.

Hampstead Norris

Although initially designated a satellite to Harwell, Hampstead Norris (Norreys) opened in the summer of 1940 to become a base for OTU day and night flying. No.15 OTU, equipped with Wellingtons, were frequent users of the base. The airfield came to the attention of the enemy on 16th September 1940 when a German aircraft dropped three bombs on the airfield causing minimal damage. The Luftwaffe did not return until April and May of 1941. It was the latter month that saw the most damage when on the 12th, ten HE and 100 incendiaries were dropped on the airfield.

At this junction of the war, a tiny island in the Mediterranean was being savagely attacked by the Regia Aeronautica and the Luftwaffe. The island was Malta and, in order to aid the defensive and offensive power in this theatre of war, many Wellington bombers were despatched from Hampstead Norris. This was a sizeable undertaking: between the 1st January and 30th June 1942, 330 Wellingtons left the airfield for overseas commitments. Further deliveries continued throughout 1942 and 1943 but in March 1944, No 15 OTU left the base, its place being taken by the Operational Refresher Training Unit. This unit was formed to give refresher courses to glider pilots destined to take part in the D-Day landings. Thirty-three Tiger Moths, nine Whitleys, twenty Albermarles and a few Horsas began to use Hampstead Norris until the 27th February 1945 when the unit moved to Matching in Essex. Reverting back to a satellite of Harwell, the Mosquitoes of No 13 OTU arrived on 15th March remaining until July when the unit left for Middleton, and Hampstead Norris was placed under Care and Maintenance. For a brief time it served as a centre for the Glider Pilot Regiment but, with the end of hostilities, no further use was made of the base.

Langley

In 1936, to cope with the increased orders for Hurricanes, the Hawker Aircraft Company of Kingston acquired land adjacent to Langley, to the east of Slough, Buckinghamshire (now Berkshire), to construct a factory and airfield. Deliveries could not have been too soon as the first off the line saw action only a couple of months after the outbreak of the war.

Initially assembling so-called 'Kingston-built' Hurricanes in conjunction with Brooklands, Langley gradually replaced Brooklands as the centre of production and was where most of the research and development flying on the Hurricane and subsequent types took place. Brooklands finally ceased production of the Hurricane in late 1942, leaving Langley to continue until July 1944 when they rolled out PZ865 – 'The Last of the Many'. The plane made numerous display appearances after the war until the inscription was removed and put on display at RAF BBMF.

After Langley came on line, testing of the new Tornado began, soon to be superseded by a much improved version called the Typhoon. Developed even further, a newer version was called the Tempest which was built in two basic versions, the Mk.V and the

Biggin Hill Heritage Hangar Hawker Hurricane. This particular aircraft was built at the Canadian works as a Sea Hurricane but never served as such. It came to the hangar in 2010 and is one of just a handful of flying Hurricanes in the world.

Mk.H, respectively powered by the Napier Sabre and the Bristol Centaurus although the latter was too late to see war service.

Langley was responsible for all the Tempests, except for the first 50 MkJIs of an order for 300 assigned to Bristol's at Banwell. The factory at Langley was still turning out both versions when the war ended, and continued until 1947.

Although Langley was technically a civilian airfield it built only military aircraft and many of the pilots employed in production testing were 'resting' RAF and Federal Aviation Administration (FAA) personnel. However the only unit to be based there that could be described as 'operational' was the flying section of the No.1 Film Production Unit, based at the nearby Pinewood Studios, and equipped with at least four Douglas Bostons. It has been said that they were responsible for most of those low level sorties over Germany at the end of the war seen in the many documentaries which starkly portray the destruction of towns and cities. They also appeared to borrow other aircraft so that a filmed record could be produced for educational purposes. This unit remained to the end of the war but flying ceased when the FPU relocated to Stanmore Park.

10
CIVILIANS AT WAR

In 1941 in a speech to the nation, Winston Churchill spoke of the risk of a forthcoming invasion.

'A Nazi invasion of Britain last autumn would have been a more or less improvised affair. Hitler took it for granted that when France gave in, we should give in. But we did not give in and he had to think again. An invasion now will be supported by a much more carefully prepared tackle and equipment, landing craft and other apparatus all of which will have been planned and manufactured during the winter months. We must all be prepared to meet gas attacks, parachute attacks and glider attacks with constancy, forethought and practised skill. In order to win the war, Hitler must destroy Great Britain.'

This is just part of one of the many speeches from the Prime Minister that rallied the civilian population. Not for them the ignominious surrender of a nation to Hitler's tyranny. They were defiant in the face of extreme danger and thus, having to suffer the Battle of Britain, the blitz and what followed, the war also became known as a 'people's war'. The words of Neville Chamberlain during 1939 had never convinced the British people that it was 'peace in our time' when they could hear on their wireless the bad news about the rest of Europe. It was obvious that London and the suburbs would be a target when eventually Hitler turned his attention to Britain. The people were not wrong.

Whilst their men were away fighting, British housewives, left to bring up the children, struggled to cope with rationing, queues and shortages. Butter, sugar, bacon and ham were the first to go on ration in 1940, followed by all meat. With these restrictions, the national diet became bread and potatoes and it was deemed a criminal offence to throw any away, however mouldy! Each shopkeeper's supplies were monitored to the amount of registered customers on his or her books and the ration book became the passport to every housewife's budget. The populace were encouraged to turn their flower gardens and lawns into vegetable patches and grow their own produce. The slogan 'Dig for Victory' appeared everywhere, with 'make do and mend' becoming the other 'in' words. The British housewife was certainly encouraged to do her bit.

The passing of the Air Raids Precaution Act in 1937 had brought with it a mass of publications to aid the general public when war eventually came. These included *Air Raid First Aid, Rescue Service Manual, First Aid and Nursing for Gas Casualties* and *Protection of your Home against Air Raids*. In addition to the many booklets, the Imperial Tobacco Company issued a set of cigarette cards giving instruction in air raid precautions. Undoubtedly the worst fear of the population was a gas attack, something that in 1939 was thought a distinct possibility. The issue of free respirators or gas masks had an alarming effect on the civilians who thought that a gas attack was imminent. Advised to carry them at all times, the fear wore off during the period of the phoney war and by the new year of 1940, people had become blasé about the whole idea, many declining to carry them at all.

With these new publications came the setting up of Civil Defence Posts for the protection of the people when away from home. Twelve regions were set up with London counting as a single region. By 1939, 1,500,000 civil defence personnel had been recruited, made up of full-time and volunteer wardens. Posts were set up throughout the capital and the suburbs, these being clearly marked and noticeable by the sand-bags surrounding them.

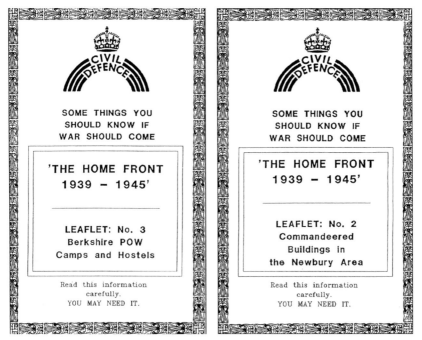

Civilians and those engaged in Civil Defence were bombarded with information and government leaflets.

During the period of the blitz they would be badly needed. The people did not need the Government to tell them that an invasion could be imminent. They only had to listen to the wireless with all the bad news from the Continent to realise that Britain was next on the enemy's list. Everywhere the message was 'don't panic', something easily said but not so easy to carry out (the expression was used as a catchphrase in the popular television series *Dad's Army*).

With so many men away on active service, many of those too young or too old, or less able, wanted to do their bit. The opportunity came on Tuesday, 14th May 1940 when the new Secretary of State, Anthony Eden broadcast an appeal.

73

'I want to speak to you tonight about the form of warfare which the Germans have been employing so extensively against Holland and Belgium. Namely the dropping of troops by parachute behind the main defensive lines. Since the war began, the Government have received countless inquiries from all over the Kingdom from men of all ages who are for one reason or another, not at present engaged in military service and who wish to do something for the defence of their country. Well, now is your opportunity. We want large numbers of such men in Great Britain who are British subjects between the ages of 17 and 65, to come forward now and offer their service in order to make assurance doubly sure. The name of the new force which is to be raised, will be the "Local Defence Volunteers".'

Within 24 hours, 250,000 men had enrolled nationally, this figure rising to more than a million by July. They were not to be known as the LDV for long. In another speech on 23rd July 1940, Winston Churchill referred to the volunteer force as the Home Guard. This name was to be officially adopted immediately after the speech.

One huge problem, however, was equipment. With the regular army needing every piece of equipment for themselves, it fell to the men of the Home Guard to train with a motley collection of impromptu weapons. Many were home-made and were in the extreme, dangerous to handle. Likewise the uniform. Initially issued with LDV and Home Guard arm-bands only, by the summer of 1940, denims became standard issue. Not until mid 1941 was the standard army battledress issued to the units. At the same time, shipments of arms from Canada and America were supplied to the Home Guard, making them at least look as though they meant business!

The main role of the volunteers was to meet the expected invasion by enemy paratroopers and to foil any invasion attempt. Together with evening and weekend training sessions came the guarding of key installations throughout the country. Railways, factories, highways and coastal protection all came under their remit and, even when it became apparent that an invasion was not imminent, the duties remained the same.

In the years when our Country

was in mortal danger

FRANK HARWOOD TREWEEKS

who served   20/5/40   to   31/12/44

gave generously of his time and

powers to make himself ready

for her defence by force of arms

and with his life if need be.

George R.I.

THE HOME GUARD

Certificates were presented to all those who served in the Home Guard.
(FH Treweeks)

As time wore on, the Home Guard did become a well organised disciplined army, with Berkshire having all units of the force on regular standby by 1941. Though the butt of many comedians' jokes, they did much for civilian morale at a very dangerous time. Had an invasion occurred, no doubt they would have given the enemy a run for his money. When the Home Guard was finally stood down in 1944, it was able to hold its head high.

As well as the Home Guard uniform, civilians were to see many foreign uniforms around their home towns, though in very confined places. A leaflet issued by the Civil Defence in Berkshire during 1940 and headed *Some things you should know if war should come*, covered several buildings and farms requisitioned for the use of prisoners of war. One of the main places was Lodge Farm Camp at Farncombe Down, Lambourn, very close to the Berkshire/Wiltshire border. It was initially requisitioned as an Italian labour camp but towards the end of the war it was considered for Germans. The camp officially opened in August 1941 and was planned to hold 500 prisoners; 120 guards were recruited but this number had to be increased within six months when the camp was expanded to house another 168 men. Further buildings were added but as an experiment, it was decided to house selected Italian POWs in Land Army hostels. These would be under the jurisdiction of the main camp and also under the command of Major R. Fidler, the Commandant. One of the main hostels was situated at Challow in Berkshire with the others based in Wiltshire. Several similar hostels were requisitioned, much to the dismay of the civilian population who did not want enemy POWs in their locality. The main sites in Berkshire were: Winter Quarter's Camp at Ascot (Camp No 7), constructed early in the war; Stratfield Mortimer (Camp No 88), built April 1943; Bradfield Road, Pangbourne, a new hostel built for 70 prisoners during 1943 and Brock Hill, Winkfield, a new hostel built for 70 prisoners.

Several other areas of Berkshire were used to aid the war effort including Newbury Racecourse which was used as an American Supply Depot and a camp for Italian and German POWs. All of these sites and many more were included in the Civil Defence leaflet.

Whilst prisoners were being sent to POW camps, children were being sent to new homes. It was known as the 'exodus of the innocents' for which there were two main reasons. The fear of bombs and gas was the first whilst the second was more for the control of the civilians by the Government. Believing that when the first bombs began to fall, the population would panic, they felt that an organised evacuation of children initially would prevent this. Friday, 1st September 1939 was the day allocated for the start of the evacuation in the south-east for schoolchildren and the elderly sick. Originally 80% of people in London had agreed that their children should be evacuated but as time wore on, only about half were willing to let their children go. However, it was still a huge operation. The first wave of evacuation consisted of 827,000 schoolchildren and 524,000 under school age accompanied by their mothers. In addition, there were 12,000 expectant mothers and 103,000 teachers and helpers. Carrying a gas mask and a rucksack and labelled with a large card stating name and age, the children were bundled onto trains, buses and coaches and sent to various 'safe' country areas. Some settled into country life quite well, others did not. For many however, it was a brief separation

With the majority of men in the armed forces, farm boys were recruited to help with the harvest.

because the expected bombing did not happen until the middle of 1940 and about three out of four evacuees had returned home to their mothers and fathers by January 1940.

For Berkshire it was not so much a case of sending children away but more of receiving them from London and the south-east. The District Council had been ordered by the Government to make a house-to-house survey of all available accommodation and to make a return to the Ministry of Health by March 1939. The Council arranged for the reception of the children and adults in village halls and schools before allocating them to a local family. Some of the children from the poorer areas of London arrived in what was termed a 'verminous condition' and really needed a lot of scrubbing before some families would accept them.

Once settled in a family, one of the greatest problems was the acute overcrowding in schools. This, plus the fact that disagreements between the local children and the evacuees were many, made it a very trying time for all. The first evacuees had been moved before the first air raid siren had sounded in anger in London and it was to be many years hence before the last of the evacuees returned home.

Before that however, the phoney war following the Munich Agreement had resulted in trenches and shelters being dug and erected all over the country. For people with gardens, the local authorities supplied them with a free Anderson shelter. Designed by an engineer named Anderson for the Home Secretary, Sir John Anderson (no relation), the instructions for self erection stated that you dug a hole 4 feet wide by 6 feet long, bolted the six pieces of corrugated iron together, tacked on the two end sections and partially covered it in earth or sand. Once erected, people tried to make it as comfortable as possible but one of the main problems was that it was liable to flood in heavy rain. A later shelter that could be used in the house was the Morrison shelter. This took the form of an iron table with mesh sides for protection from flying bricks or glass should a bomb hit the house. Usually placed in the lounge, it could be used as a table for eating off and as a bed to sleep under. As an infant, yours truly had many a good night's sleep under such a shelter!

When the bombing of towns and cities began, the wailing of the sirens forced the civilian population to take cover in whatever way possible. Under the stairs, out to the shelters, down to the underground stations where possible or to the communal shelters provided by the local authorities. In order to convey to the reader the strain that this was to put the civilians under, the following incidents are worth recording and are but a few of the many.

In Newbury, the sirens sounded on 244 occasions with the first on Tuesday, 25th June 1940 at 1.15 am and the last on 29th August 1944. The 'alerts' occupied a period of time amounting to 24,030

An all too familiar scene – a building 'well alight' after a Luftwaffe raid. (J Chaffey)

minutes with the peak period during the winter of 1940 and the following spring. The town itself experienced three bad bombing attacks, each of which happened on a Wednesday. The first two caused a considerable amount of damage but no deaths. This was to come on the third occasion, the results of which shook the people of Newbury and of Berkshire as a whole.

As 10th February 1943 dawned, the people of the town woke to an overcast day. By midday the cloud appeared to be lifting and by tea-time, there were definite breaks and signs of blue skies. Being a Wednesday, most of the shops were shut for half day but the town was still busy. At around 4.35 pm, people looked up as the sound of aircraft engines was heard. What they did not see was a lone Dornier 217E of KG40 approaching the town. It was a low-level attack which within minutes caused both death and massive destruction to a community. Dropping eight high explosive bombs on the south side of Newbury, St John's church, the senior council school and ten houses were reduced to rubble. Many more

Lone Dornier 217Es dropped bombs on Newbury and Reading on 10th February 1943. (MAP)

Scenes of devastation after a bomb landed on the People's Pantry in Reading on 10th February 1943, killing and maiming civilians. (Berkshire Chronicle via D Chamberlain)

buildings close by were damaged, some beyond repair, with many people becoming homeless in minutes. Of greater consequence, however, was the loss of life and terrible injuries. Nineteen people perished in the raid with dozens more injured.

The aircraft had approached from the low cloud base over Wash Water. It crossed Monks Lane and Meadow Road, strafing the streets with machine gun fire as it did so. Just over the cemetery in Newtown Road, the first bombs fell. Many assumed it was a friendly aircraft and came out of their houses to look up. The first bomb ripped through the houses in Southampton Terrace. It landed in the middle and exploded, killing three women. The second bomb tore through the roof of a building and continued to explode in St John's church, ripping it apart. Fortunately the church was empty with the exception of one of the church workers who was in the vestry at the time. Luckily she escaped with just minor injuries. Further bombs passed through another set of houses in Madeira Place and exploded in a set of almshouses with a terrible loss of life. Another bomb hit the senior council school and whilst luckily most of the children had gone home, three were still on the premises and were killed.

It was Newbury's darkest hour. After the noise of the exploding bombs, for seconds a poignant silence remained until the screams and cries of the dying and injured were heard. Less than a week after the tragedy, a funeral service was held at Shaw cemetery for 13 of the dead, all of them being buried in a communal grave. This was because it had been found impossible to identify certain bodies.

Twenty miles to the east on the same day, another single Dornier bomber again came in fast and low to wreak devastation and death on an innocent civilian population. Like Newbury, in Reading town centre it was early closing day. Despite this, lots of people were out and about in the cold but bright weather. The teashops such as the 'People's Pantry', were full of customers enjoying a quiet tea. The People's Pantry was one of a chain of what were called British Restaurants. These were communal kitchens designed to help feed those who had run out of ration coupons, been bombed, or otherwise needed help. It was Churchill

St Laurence's church, Reading after the Dornier attack. It was the last of a stick of four bombs that caused the damage. (Berkshire Chronicle via D Chamberlain)

who coined the name 'British Restaurants'. They were cheap, run by volunteers, and extremely popular. Suddenly, at around 4.35 pm, the quiet was shattered as the staccato sound of machine-gun fire was heard followed by three distinct explosions. This was followed by more gunfire as a Dornier 217 swooped low over the town before climbing away leaving a trail of devastation.

The first bomb had dropped on the Heelas Garage in Minster Street demolishing the premises and those either side of it plus several cars. The second came down on a department store which, whilst extensively damaged, incurred no loss of life though several female staff living on the premises were injured. It was however, the third that caused the destruction and many deaths. It fell fairly and squarely on the 'People's Pantry'. As the sounds of the first two explosions were heard, many of the customers began to make their way to the door to see what had happened outside. As they did so, the roof fell in as the bomb exploded throwing pieces of red hot metal into flesh and furniture alike. All the customers and staff were instantly buried beneath the rubble of brick and plaster. As the aircraft continued to drop a further bomb next to the church of St Laurence, the noise of its engines and this last explosion helped to block out the cries of the dying and injured.

As the Dornier 217 continued to climb away, 41 people were left dead with over 100 injured, some very badly. Of the 86 casualties taken to Reading Hospital, one was found dead on arrival, 42 were admitted to the emergency Benyon Ward and the remainder were treated in the casualty department, including Michael Bond, the creator of 'Paddington Bear'. Thirty-one required amputations and six people were so seriously injured that they needed urgent blood transfusions. Three surgeons operated continuously and within seven and a half hours, all the casualties had been dealt with. All the hospital supply of blood had been required and the following day, the donors were recalled and the stock replenished. The search for survivors went long into the night and the next day, with the ARP workers toiling to remove debris with their bare hands. They were assisted by all the emergency services but by the afternoon of the next day, all hopes of finding anyone else alive had gone. For one 14-year-old who experienced the terror and was badly injured in the attack, it was something he would never forget.

'Wednesday the 10th was cold and at 4.30 I was waiting for a friend who like myself had just left school. We were both due to start work the next week. As he was late at the meeting place, I went next door to a British Restaurant to get a cup of tea to warm me up. When I went in, there were about 30 people inside. I finished my tea, lit a cigarette and wandered outside walking about 20 yards to the entrance of the arcade which was glass roofed and very old. I didn't hear the sirens sounding but all of a sudden there were three or four explosions and as I looked up, I actually saw a bomb falling. It landed a few yards from where I was standing and as I turned to run, I was blown about 20 yards through the arcade and lay there in the eerie silence.

'Although my ears were ringing, I could still hear the occasional fall of masonry and glass. I cannot remember much after that except waking up in hospital with a fractured skull, broken right femur, broken arm and shrapnel in my back, legs and head. In all I spent eight months in hospital. It really was a bad day for all the people and having researched the incident thoroughly, one person involved was an American serviceman. He was badly injured protecting his English girl-friend and through my research over the years, I was able to go to America in 1996 to meet him once again. I do not think that anyone who was in that attack will ever forget that day.'

Derek Chamberlain was just one of the many injured and was indeed lucky that he did not lose his life. Of those who did, several were buried on Tuesday, 16th February. In a harrowing scene, the remains were interred in the presence of weeping relatives and friends. An early hour had been selected with a view to keeping away sightseers. The bodies were enclosed in coffins of unpolished elm and the graves were draped in purple, floral tributes being placed at the head of each. One grave contained two unidentified bodies and another, the separate coffins of two little children. A large floral cross, composed of carnations, daffodils and arum lilies and inscribed 'From the Corporation, to express the sympathy of the towns-people' was placed on end in the centre. A further cross carried the message, 'as a small tribute from the WVS'.

With the burials over, Reading got back to business. Many people wondered just why such a raid had taken place over a non-military town. Or was it non-military? For 50 years after the event, it was still assumed that the pilot simply picked the town at random to drop his bombs, and machine-gun buildings and innocent civilians. No official explanation was forthcoming until 1993 when research revealed that it may not have been a random target. It had been realised early in the war that the high power BBC transmitters would provide radio navigational aids for enemy aircraft. In order to deny the enemy this facility, it was decided that each town with a population of 50,000 or more would receive a low powered transmitter from which to hear the BBC Home Service. Codenamed 'Group H', 61 of these stations were secretly

An intact V1 is on display at the Imperial War Museum in London.

opened with Reading being Station 19. It began operations on 5th May 1941 and it was housed inside the 'People's Pantry'. After the war most Group H transmitters were quietly scrapped except a few which were retained for local radio. Was it a coincidence that the 'Pantry' received a direct hit or did the German intelligence service excel itself on this occasion?

The attacks upon civilian targets by loan raiders in daylight caused the population much distress. The Home Counties were only a short distance from air bases in France and they were particularly at risk up to the end of 1943. However, the terror from the skies did not end there as the next year saw the even more deadly 'revenge' weapons, the V1 'doodlebug' and then the enormous V2 rocket. The doodlebug you could at least see and hear. The V2 rocket literally fell out of the sky and exploded with huge force before you were aware of it at all. So both these weapons brought considerable suffering and damage to the area and to an unsuspecting public. Whilst the aiming point for the V1 was the Tower of London, some travelled further and landed in all the Home Counties. Berkshire was fortunate in being a good way west of London. Other counties, especially Middlesex, were not so lucky.

Monday, 19th June 1944, six days after the first V1 had been launched, one of the rockets came down at Heston. The morning dawned clear but windy. An alert at 06.25 turned out to be a large formation of B-17s outward bound but just before 8 am, a V1 landed in a neat cul-de-sac near Vicarage Farm Road. The owner of one of the houses, Mr Senior, happened to be looking through his kitchen window when he saw the V1 approaching. To his horror he saw the flame from the tail splutter and at the top of his voice shouted, 'That's for us'. Rushing out to the Anderson shelter, he barely made it before the blast from the explosion helped him through the entrance.

Nearby, another neighbour was asleep when the V1 came down. The double bed in which he was sleeping was split down the middle by the blast, with the mattress luckily wrapping itself around him and saving him from personal injury. At the same time, the debris and dust from the roof and ceiling fell into the

A V2 rocket is prepared for launch. (Flight)

bedroom. The two occupants of the house, together with others made homeless, were taken to the Congregational church where their cuts and bruises were attended to. The village hall in Heston was also requisitioned for people made homeless and for the treatment of minor injuries. The rocket, which had landed in the road, caused three deaths with the destruction of almost 1,300 houses around St Leonard's Gardens. A second V1, that came down ten days later in fields at the end of Lampton Avenue, caused only minor casualties and damaged 350 houses. This was because the second bomb came down in a field which absorbed the impact whereas the first exploded on concrete.

Between July and August, three V1s fell on nearby Brentford with the first sadly killing five people. It was however, on 22nd February 1945 that the first V2 fell on the Heston and Isleworth district. A report in the *Daily Herald* dated Saturday, 11th November 1944 said it all on the front page: 'Comets that dive from 70 miles. Britain's front line at home is under fire again from a stratosphere rocket that is dropping on us from 60 to 70 miles up in the air, a rocket that travels faster than sound and flashes across the sky like a "comet trailing fire". There is no warning, no siren, no time to take shelter. For this is the most indiscriminate weapon of this or any other war. It is a sinister, eerie form of war.'

The first fell beside St Helen's House, completely demolishing the house together with damage to many others. Thirty minor injuries were treated at the local reception centre. It was however, the second V2 to come down within the Heston district that caused the largest number of casualties. It fell at 9.39 am on Wednesday, 21st March 1945 onto the Packard engine factory on the Great West Road. Within minutes of the explosion, the rescue services were on the scene but a large fire that was burning at the site prevented any immediate clearance work. This was brought under control with the arrival of the NFS with about 20 vehicles.

The V2 had landed fairly and squarely on the factory, which was producing marine engines. With about 100 men on the shop floor at the time, the entire roof collapsed onto them burying them in brick and corrugated metal. As soon as they were able, the rescue parties moved in and with bare hands, began searching the rubble for survivors. The final toll was 32 killed, 102 seriously injured and 390 slightly injured. Together with Packards, several other factories within the locality were damaged. A few days after the incident the area was visited by the king and queen who talked to the workforce and their families and expressed dismay and sympathy at the dreadful loss of life.

These incidents are but a few in what, for the civilian population, was a time of terror. On 2nd August 1944 Winston Churchill gave a report to Parliament at which he said the total number of V1s, named 'Divers', sent to Britain was then 5,735 which had killed 4,335 people. A later report stated in addition, 1,115 V2s, named 'Big Ben', were fired at Britain which had killed 2,612 people in London alone. There were many others in rural areas. According to official records, Berkshire received two V1 attacks whilst next door Buckinghamshire received 27.

APPENDIX

THE SQUADRONS AND UNITS OF THE ROYAL AIR FORCE AND UNITED STATES ARMY AIR FORCE THAT WERE BASED AT AIRFIELDS IN BERKSHIRE

ALDERMASTON: Station 467 – 60th TCG, 315th TCG, 370th FG, 434th TCG.

GREAT SHEFFORD – RLG for No 8 EFTS.

GREENHAM COMMON: Station 486 – 51st TCW, 354th FG, 368th FG, 438th TCG, 316th Group.

MEMBURY: Station 466 – 3rd Photographic, 67th Observation Group, 6th Tactical Air Depot, 366th FG, 436th TCG, 525 Squadron RAF, 187 Squadron RAF.

THEALE – 26 EFTS, 128 Glider Squadron.

WELFORD: Station 474 – 315th TCG, 434th TCG, 435th TCG, 90th TCS, 100th Regional Support Group, 20th FW.

WHITE WALTHAM – No 13 E&RFTS, No 13 EFTS, No 3 Ferry Pilots School, No 1 Ferry Pilots School.

WINKFIELD – RLG for No 18 EFTS.

WOODLEY – No 8 E&RFTS, No 8 EFTS, No 10 FIS, No 8 Reserve Flying School.

ACKNOWLEDGEMENTS

I acknowledge with thanks all the individuals and organisations who have assisted me in the writing of this book: Mrs Mary Ellis; Mr Peter Baker; Mr Derek Chamberlain; Mrs Edie Mullins; Miss Pamela Froom; Mr Leonard Lean; Mrs Eileen Snelling; Dr Chris Samson; Mr Len Pilkington; Mr Roger A. Freeman; Mr Cecil G. Curran; Mr Anthony J. King; Mr James Marshall; Mrs Margaret Carruthers; Mrs Mavis Dyson; Mr Bert Shrimpton; WO J. Wilcox, *Newbury Weekly News*; Reading Newspaper Series; US Air Force Historical Research Agency; RAF Museum; Imperial War Museum; Air Historical Branch, MOD; Public Records Office, Kew; Mr James Hampton; and James Marshall.

If I have omitted to mention any person or organisation or incorrectly credited any photographs, please accept my sincere apologies. Final thanks go to my wife, Barbara, for her patience when spending long evenings alone and for her correcting skills.

BIBLIOGRAPHY

During my research I consulted various other works. I list them below with grateful thanks to the authors.

Ashworth, Chris, *Action Stations 9*, Patrick Stephens 1985.
Bowyer, Chaz, *Fighter Command 1936/68*, Sphere Books 1981.
Bowyer, Michael J.F., *Action Stations 6*, Patrick Stephens 1983.
Chiltern Aviation Society, *From Airships to Concorde*.
Collier, Richard, *Eagle Day*, Pan Books 1968.
Congdon, Philip, *Per Ardua ad Astra*, Airlife 1987.
Freeman, Roger A., *Airfields of the Eighth*, Battle of Britain Prints Int Ltd 1978.
Freeman, Roger A., *Airfields of the Ninth*, Battle of Britain Prints Int Ltd 1992.
Gardiner, Juliet, *The People's War*, Select Editions 1991.
Halley, James J., *Squadrons of the RAF*, Air Britain 1980.
Halpenny, Bruce Barrymore, *Action Stations 8*, Patrick Stephens 1984.
Jackson, Robert, *Spitfire-The Combat History*, Airlife 1995.
Jefford MBE, W/Cdr C.G., *RAF Squadrons*, Airlife.
Ramsey, Winston G., *The Battle of Britain Then and Now*, Battle of Britain Prints Int Ltd 1980.
Ramsey, Winston G., *The Blitz – Then and Now*, Battle of Britain Prints Int Ltd 1979.

Rawlings, John, *Fighter Squadrons of the RAF*, Macdonald & Co 1968.

Robinson, Anthony, *RAF Fighter Squadrons in the Battle of Britain*, Brockhampton Press 1987.

Ross DFC, Tony, *75 Eventful Years A Tribute to the RAF*, Wingham Aviation Books 1991.

Smith, David, *Britain's Military Airfields 1939/45*, Patrick Stephens 1989.

Wright, Robert, *Dowding and the Battle of Britain*, Corgi 1970.

INDEX

95